21st Century
Junior Library

WHAT IS DISABILITY?

Erin Hawley

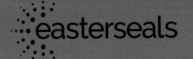
easterseals

Understanding Disability

Published in the United States of America by:

CHERRY LAKE PRESS
2395 South Huron Parkway, Suite 200, Ann Arbor, Michigan 48104
www.cherrylakepress.com

Reading Adviser: Beth Walker Gambro, MS, Ed., Reading Consultant, Yorkville, IL

Photo Credits: © Pixel-Shot/Shutterstock.com, cover, 1; © wavebreakmedia/Shutterstock.com, 5;
© Goldsithney/Shutterstock.com, 6; © Art_Photo/Shutterstock.com, 7; © Ivan_Shenets/Shutterstock.com, 8 [left];
© Click and Photo/Shutterstock.com, 8 [right]; © Olesia Bilkei/Shutterstock.com, 9; © BAZA Production/
Shutterstock.com, 10, 11; © karelnoppe/Shutterstock.com, 12; © Jaren Jai Wicklund/Shutterstock.com, 13;
© insta_photos/Shutterstock.com, 14; © Bangkok Click Studio/Shutterstock.com, 17; © Denis Kuvaev/
Shutterstock.com, 18; © AnnGaysorn/Shutterstock.com, 20; © MadPixel/Shutterstock.com, 21

Cherry Lake Press is an imprint of Cherry Lake Publishing Group.

Library of Congress Cataloging-in-Publication Data
Names: Hawley, Erin, author.
Title: What is disability? / by Erin Hawley.
Description: Ann Arbor, Michigan : Cherry Lake Publishing, [2022] | Series: Understanding disability |
    Includes bibliographical references. | Audience: Grades 2-3
Identifiers: LCCN 2022005403 | ISBN 9781668910689 (paperback) | ISBN 9781668909089 (hardcover) |
    ISBN 9781668912270 (ebook) | ISBN 9781668913864 (pdf)
Subjects: LCSH: People with disabilities—Juvenile literature. | Disabilities—Juvenile literature.
Classification: LCC HV1568 .H3964 2022 | DDC 362.4—dc23/eng/20220210
LC record available at https://lccn.loc.gov/2022005403

Cherry Lake Press would like to acknowledge the work of the Partnership for 21st Century Learning, a Network
of Battelle for Kids. Please visit http://www.battelleforkids.org/networks/p21 for more information.

Printed in the United States of America
Corporate Graphics

Easterseals is enriching education through greater disability equity, inclusion and access. Join us at www.Easterseals.com.

CONTENTS

WHAT IS DISABILITY?

Disability is a physical, mental, or emotional difference that affects a person's **ability** to do everyday tasks. These tasks might include walking, talking, seeing, hearing, dressing themselves, solving a puzzle, or staying calm. Disability can make thousands of other tasks difficult without support, but disability isn't a bad thing! It's just a normal difference that one in four people have.

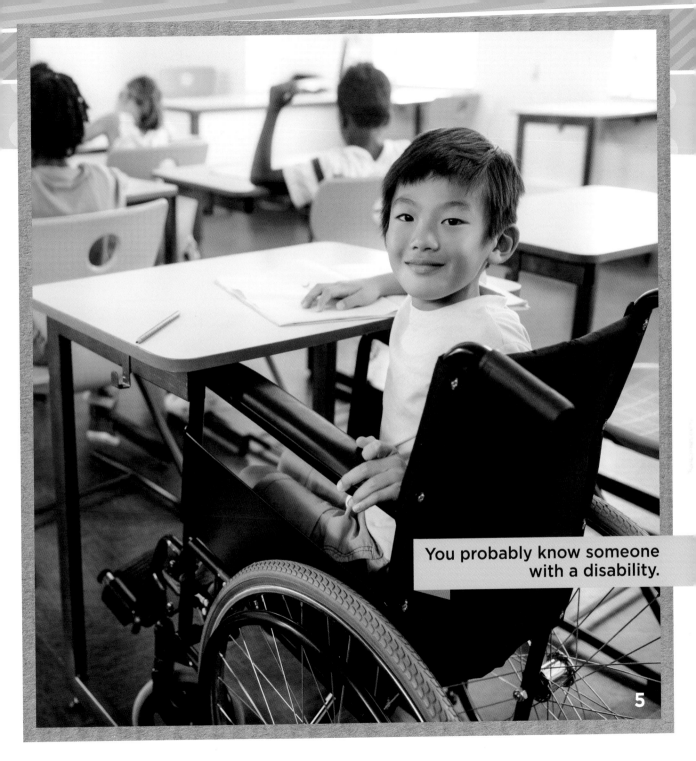

You probably know someone with a disability.

Humans are all different, which is pretty cool. The world would be a boring place if everyone was the same, right?

Disability is usually understood as a **medical diagnosis**. Have you ever gone to the doctor? When you're sick, the doctor can *name* whatever it is that's making you sick, like the flu or chicken pox. That *name* is a medical diagnosis!

A medical diagnosis may sound scary, but it doesn't have to be!

A person with a disability also has a name for their disability. For example, someone who can't hear is Deaf or hard of hearing. Someone who has trouble reading could have **dyslexia**. Someone using a wheelchair could have **cerebral palsy**. Thousands of different disabilities exist.

Someone with a disability can have an illness, such as **diabetes**. But that doesn't mean people with disabilities are always sick or feel bad. Just like everyone else, people with disabilities have good days and bad days! Some disabled people never feel sick, but their different way of doing something still means they have a disability. For example, someone who is Deaf isn't sick—they just can't hear.

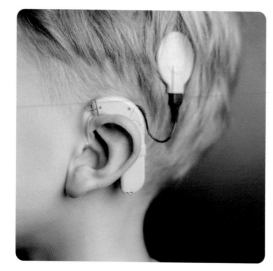
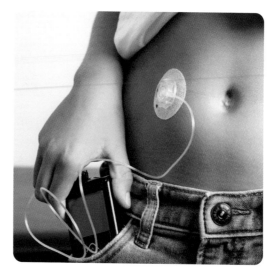

Disabilities aren't **contagious**. You can't catch someone else's disability like you can catch a cold. Also, some disabilities may be temporary. Other people may have their disability for their entire lives.

Make a Guess!

Now that you know what a medical diagnosis is, what are some other diagnoses that you can think of?

DISABILITY AND IDENTITY

Even though disability is often a medical diagnosis, it can also be an important part of someone's **identity**. That means they consider their disability an important part of who they are. Think of it this way—what is something that makes you, *you*?

Think!

Think about all the identities you and your friends have. What are your favorite parts about being you? What do you like about your friends?

Your name is part of your identity, just like your family, hair color, and whether you wear glasses or not. Having a disability is not something to be ashamed or scared of. It's just an important part of who you are! You don't have to feel uncomfortable around someone with a disability. Remember that everyone is different, so just treat

Look!

The next time you meet someone with a disability, what are some ways you can show them respect?

someone with a disability like you would treat someone without a disability! As long as you treat people with respect, your friend circle will grow— and who doesn't want more friends?

What's something you like to do with your friends?

You can't always tell if someone has a disability just by looking at them.

WHAT DOES DISABILITY LOOK LIKE?

You probably know someone with a disability, even if you can't tell by looking at them. That's because there are visible disabilities and invisible disabilities. When you can see someone using a wheelchair or walker, or if you see someone without an arm or hand, these are *visible* disabilities. Visible just means that you can see or understand something by looking at it. But not all disabilities are so obvious. Someone who has trouble learning in school may not look like they have a disability, but they do. When you can't see someone's disability, it means they have an invisible disability.

As we learned earlier, people with disabilities can have good days and bad days. For example, they may have days when they can walk just fine. Other days, they may have to use a wheelchair or cane. And some people can't walk at all. These people have to use a wheelchair all the time, and that's okay.

Ask Questions!

If you think someone may have a disability, it's okay to ask questions to better understand them. Remember it's important to show respect. How would you ask questions respectfully?

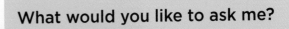

What would you like to ask me?

Even someone who can't walk at all can still get out of their wheelchair with help from another person or an **assistive device**.

It's also important to know that a disability can be something you are born with or something you **acquire** later in life. You can be any age and have a disability!

Create!

Remember we said it's good to ask questions if you don't understand something? Make a list of five questions you have about disability and search online with an adult for the answers to your questions. There is lots more to learn about disability!

EXTEND YOUR LEARNING

Think of someone in your life who has a visible or invisible disability. Write down three things about them—like their eye color, favorite animal, favorite sports team—or anything else you want. Make the same list for yourself. How are you different from each other and how are you alike? Think about everything we learned as you write about this person.

GLOSSARY

ability (uh-BIH-luh-tee) being able to do something, such as walk or read

acquire (uh-KWYR) to get or learn something

assistive device (uh-SIH-stiv dih-VYS) an object that can help a disabled person navigate their environment, such as a grab bar, wheelchair, lift, or accessible gaming controller

cerebral palsy (suh-REE-bruhl PAHL-zee) a type of disability that can affect your ability to move, walk, or speak

contagious (kuhn-TAY-juhs) able to be transmitted from one person to another

diabetes (dye-uh-BEE-teez) a disability that affects your body's ability to manage your blood sugar

dyslexia (dis-LEK-see-uh) a disability that affects a person's ability to read words on a page, making reading difficult

identity (eye-DEN-tuh-tee) the things that make who you are

medical diagnosis (MEH-duh-kuhl dye-ig-NOH-suhs) the name of an illness or disability

respect (rih-SPEKT) treating someone with kindness and understanding

FIND OUT MORE

Books

Burcaw, Shane. *Not So Different: What You Really Want to Ask about Having a Disability.* New York, NY: Roaring Brook Press, 2017.

Burnell, Cerrie. *I Am Not a Label: 34 Disabled Artists, Thinkers, Athletes and Activists from Past and Present.* London, UK: Wide Eyed Editions, 2020.

Websites

Get Involved with Easterseals
https://www.easterseals.com/get-involved
Learn about the different ways you can get involved in increasing opportunities for people with disabilities, from advocacy to volunteering.

YouTube—My Medical Story: Nikki Lilly
https://youtu.be/dop6JIlBtec
Nikki Lilly talks about what it's like living with an arteriovenous malformation (AVM).

YouTube—What Does it Feel Like to be Disabled?
https://youtu.be/TTYI35ldRWU
Listen to Shane talk about what it's like to have a disability and why it's not a bad thing.

INDEX

ABOUT THE AUTHOR

Erin Hawley is a writer and content creator with muscular dystrophy and anxiety. Her work focuses on accessibility and disability representation in technology. She has worked with companies like Microsoft, Logitech, Adobe, and Electronic Arts to ensure that accessibility and inclusivity is not an afterthought. Erin has been featured in *The New York Times, USA Today, HuffPost*, and other publications. She lives in Keyport, New Jersey, and you can usually find her editing videos for her YouTube channel or with her nose in a book. Currently, she works as a communications and digital content producer for Easterseals National Office.